W9-DDZ-912

Making Books A to Z

Illustrator:
Barb Lorseyedi

Editor:
Stephanie Buehler, M.P.W., M.A.

Editorial Project Manager:
Ina Massler Levin, M.A.

Editor-in-Chief:
Sharon Coan, M.S. Ed.

Art Director:
Elayne Roberts

Associate Designer:
Denise Bauer

Cover Artist:
Larry Bauer

Product Manager:
Phil Garcia

Imaging:
David Bennett
Alfred Lau

Publishers:
Rachelle Cracchiolo, M.S. Ed.
Mary Dupuy Smith, M.S. Ed.

Author:

by Jill Gasquet

Teacher Created Materials, Inc.
P.O. Box 1040
Huntington Beach, CA 92647
ISBN-1-55734-049-8

©1996 Teacher Created Materials, Inc.   Made in U.S.A.

990400

29209

ABCDEFGHIJKLMNOPQRSTUVWXYZ

Table of Contents

ABCDEFGHIJKLMNOPQRSTUVWXYZ

Introduction

Traditionally, instruction in language arts skills progresses from part to whole, that is, from letter to sound, sound to word, word to sentence, and finally, sentence to story. Whole language instruction reverses this process; skill learning begins with a story and then progresses to sentences, words, sounds, and letters. This book uses a combination of both methods in its use of both literature and thematic units centered around recognition of letters and their accompanying sounds. Students will also learn word recognition, syntax, and spelling.

Making Big Books A to Z can be adapted for use with readers and writers at various stages of development. Pre-readers and writers can dictate their ideas to the teacher, contribute to lists, illustrate sentence patterns, use word cards, and perform choral readings. Beginning writers will be able to progress from labeling pictures to writing sentences.

For each letter of the alphabet, *Making Big Books A to Z* suggests two ideas for big books. Each big book alphabet lesson provides an objective, motivation, sample sentence pattern, ideas for illustrations, recommendations for the form of publication, and suggested reading vocabulary. Student response pages follow the lesson outline.

Overview of the Process

- Listen to a story, rhyme, or song.

- Discuss the thematic unit and then brainstorm and list related ideas.

- Create big book contributions using the suggested sentence patterns. Depending upon students' development, they can either dictate needed words to the teacher, or they may write words independently.

- Student work should be rewritten on heavy paper or poster board for big book pages. Laminating student pages is optional.

- Students can then illustrate their big book pages.

- Compile the student pages into a big book. Add an illustrated poster cover.

Introduction (cont.)

- The big book can be sewn together with large needle and heavy-duty thread or dental floss. (Use a thimble!) The big book also can be bound using yarn, metal rings, or strips of colored cloth tape (available at large stationery stores).

- Make word cards and/or sentence strips to accompany the big book. Place them into plastic bags that will be taped or stapled inside the big book's cover.

Suggestions for Using Big Books

- Read the big book to the class.

- Have students read the big book along with the teacher.

- Students can match word cards and/or sentence strips with text in the big book.

- Use the big book to emphasize phonics, punctuation, or reading strategy currently being studied.

- Display the big book in the classroom for student use.

Sending the Big Books Home

- Children may take turns taking big books home. Reproduce the Letter to Parents on page 5, fill in the students' names, and affix a copy to the back of the big book for parents to read and sign.

- Use the form on page 6 to record the students' names and dates of check-out. Check off students' names when they have returned the book.

- Protect the books by sending them home wrapped in a large plastic bag. Do not send books home on bad weather days.

- Circulate another big book only when the previous book has been returned.

- Send home a reminder if the book is overdue.

- Check the big books when returned, and repair if necessary. Replace any missing word cards or sentence strips.

- Accept that a book may be lost or destroyed. The benefits of using big books are worth the risk of loss.

A B C D E F G H I J K L M N O P Q R S T U V W X Y Z

Dear Parents,

We would like to share the big book we made together in our classroom. Ideas for using this book are the following:

- Read the book to your child.

- Let your child read along with you.

- Match sentence strips and/or word cards.

- Let your child point out words he or she knows.

- Point out letters of the alphabet and say the sound of the letter.

Please sign your name on the line beside your child's name and return the big book on the next school day. Thank you.

Student	Parent Signature
_____	_____
_____	_____
_____	_____
_____	_____
_____	_____
_____	_____
_____	_____
_____	_____
_____	_____
_____	_____
_____	_____
_____	_____
_____	_____
_____	_____
_____	_____

ABCDEFGHIJKLMNOPQRSTUVWXYZ

Big Book Check-out List

Week of_____

Book	Monday Name	✓	Tuesday Name	✓	Wednesday Name	✓	Thursday Name	✓	Friday Name	✓

The Letter A

What Is an Apple?

Objective: Recognize **Aa** and the short a sound; discuss apples.

Motivation: Students will listen to stories and poems about apples such as "Apple Tree! Apple Tree!" by Mary Blocksma.

Written Expression: Students will complete the following sentence pattern on page 8:

An apple is ___.

Illustration: Students will use crayons or markers to draw an apple below the sentence pattern.

Publication: Create an apple-shaped wheel book. Cut out a large apple from red or green poster board. On the outer edge, cut a box to display the sentence patterns. Then, cut within the apple a smaller box that will display the students' names. Next, make a large wheel which will fit behind the apple. Glue the students' sentence patterns around the wheel edge. Write the students' names to correspond to the sentence patterns so that their display is coordinated as the wheel is turned. Attach the apple wheel and display wheel with a paper fastener.

Reading Skills: Write word cards for an, apple, is, and what. For more advanced readers, make word cards with adjectives.

A Is for Ape and Animals

Objective: Recognize **Aa** and the long a sound; learn animal names

Motivation: Students will listen to animal stories and look at pictures of animals.

Written Expression: Students will complete the following sentence pattern on page 9:

This is a (n)___.

Illustration: Print **A** or **a** on one piece of art paper per student. Using crayons or markers, students will create real or fantasy animals, using the letter form as a base for their drawings.

Publication: Compile the students' work into a big book displaying an ape on the cover.

Reading Skills: Write word cards for A, is, for, ape, and animals. For more advanced readers, write animal name cards.

Name _____

What is an apple?
An apple is _____

8

Name _____

A is for ape and other animals.

This is a(n) _____ .

The Letter B

I See a Bird

Objective: Recognize **Bb** and the b sound; brainstorm and list words describing birds and their activities.

Motivation: Listen to bird stories and poems and look at bird pictures. Brainstorm and list words that describe birds and what they do.

Written Expression: Students will complete the following sentence pattern on page 11:

I see a bird and the bird sees me.

The bird is_____.

The bird has_____.

The bird can_____.

I see a bird and the bird sees me.

Illustration: Students will draw pictures of birds, depicting the creative pattern of the birds' feathers.

Publication: Complete bird pop-up books (page 12). Compile and add the children's work for table-top display.

Reading Skills: Write sentence strips for each part of the pattern:

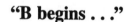

"B begins . . ."

Objective: Recognize **Bb** and the b sound; study bears

Motivation: Listen to *The Berenstains' B Book* by Stan and Jan Berenstain. Brainstorm and list words beginning with the b sound.

Written Expression: Students will use the "_____ begins with B" pattern on page 13.

Illustration: On B-shaped art paper, ask the children to draw B pictures that complement their pattern sentences.

Publication: Compile the students' work into a big book with a B-shaped cover.

Reading Skills: Write matching word cards for "B begins" and B words used by students.

Name _____

I see a bird and the bird sees me.

The bird is _____ .

The bird has _____ .

The bird can _____ .

I see a bird and the bird sees me.

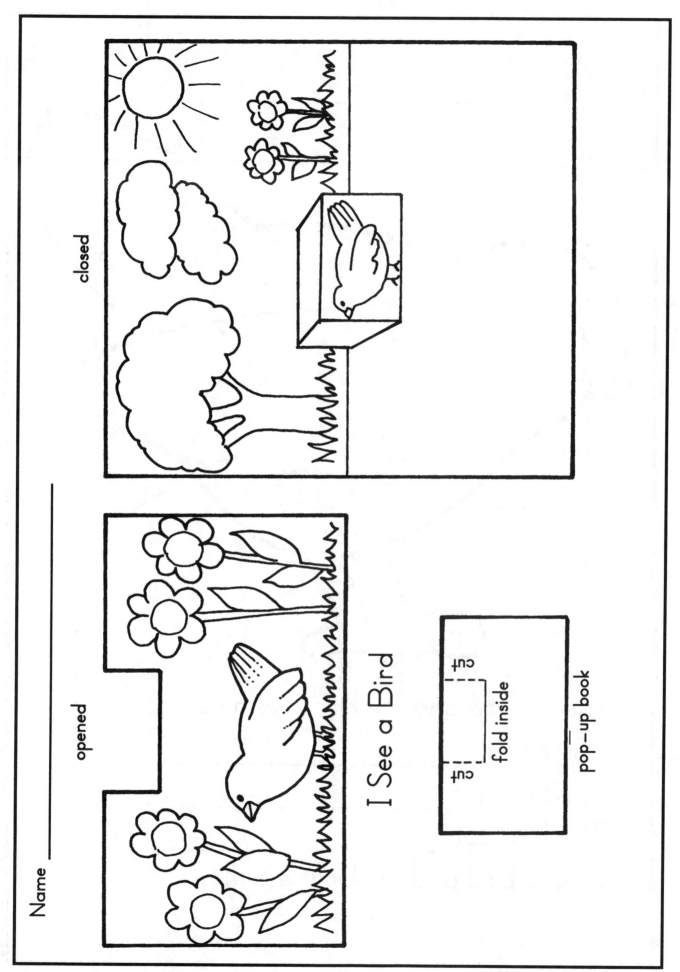

closed

opened

Name _____

I See a Bird

cut

fold inside

cut

pop-up book

Name _____

B

_____ begins with B.

The Letter C

My Cat Can . . .

Objective: Recognize Cc and its sound; learn about cats.

Motivation: Listen to *The Cat in the Hat* by Dr. Seuss. Brainstorm and list words that portray how cats look and act. Sing the song, "My Cat Is Bigger Than your Cat." Choose other words to replace the underlined word.

Written Expression: Students complete the following sentence pattern on page 15:

My cat is ___ than your cat.

My cat is ___ than yours.

My cat is ___.

It can ____.

My cat is ___ than yours.

Illustration: Direct students to color or paint cat-shaped paper.

Publication: Compile pupils' cat-shaped papers into a big book with a cat-shaped cover.

Reading Skills: Write sentence strips for "My cat is ___ than your cat," and "It can ___." Write word cards for student-supplied words.

Clifford Goes to...

Objective: Recognize Cc and its sound; read "Clifford" stories

Motivation: Listen to "Clifford" book collections by Norman Bridwell.

Written Expression: Students will dictate an original Clifford story such as "Clifford Goes to School" or "Clifford Goes to (name of state)" using page 16.

Illustration: After the original story is written in short portions on art paper, students will illustrate it with crayons or markers.

Publication: Compile the students' work in the correct order of the story. Add a student-drawn cover of Clifford.

Reading Skills: Write word cards for c words used in the "Clifford" stories the students have written.

Name _____

My Cat

My cat is _____

than your cat.

My cat is _____

than yours.

My cat is _____.

It can _____.

My cat is _____

than yours.

Name _____

Clifford, the Big Red Dog _____

_____

The Letter D

In Dinosaur Days

Objective: Recognize **Dd** and its sound; study dinosaurs.

Motivation: Listen to dinosaur stories and facts.

Written Expression: Ask students to write or dictate an ending for the story starter, "In dinosaur days . . . " on an outlined picture of a dinosaur (pages 18-20).

Illustration: Students can create a crayon rubbing of dinosaurs, plants, mountains, volcanoes and clouds. For this activity, prepare cutouts of these items from sandpaper. Students can then arrange their chosen sandpaper on the sticky side of a sheet of contact paper. Then use a second sheet of contact paper to sandwich the cutouts in between. The contact paper holds the cutouts in place and can be reused. Place art paper over the cutouts and rub the paper with the side of the crayons to make the rubbing appear.

Publication: Collate students' artwork with their dinosaur stories. Then, compile them into a big book with a dinosaur crayon rubbing cover.

Reading Skills: Write word cards for dinosaur, in, and days, plus any words repeated often in the student-related stories.

Some Dogs . . . Some Do Not

Objective: Recognize **Dd** and its sound; learn about dogs' behavior.

Motivation: Listen to books about dogs, such as *Henry, the Dirty Dog* by Gene Zion and *The Digging-est Dog* by Al Perkins. Discuss pictures of dogs. Brainstorm and list things that dogs can do.

Written Expression: Students will complete the following sentence pattern on page 21:

Some dogs bark very loudly.
Some do not.
What kind of dog would you like?

_____

Illustration: Students draw pictures of dogs to accompany their completed sentence patterns.

Publication: Compile the students' work into a book with a cover showing dogs in various activities.

Reading Skills: Write word cards for the sentence pattern and any other frequently used words.

Name _____

In Dinosaur Days

18

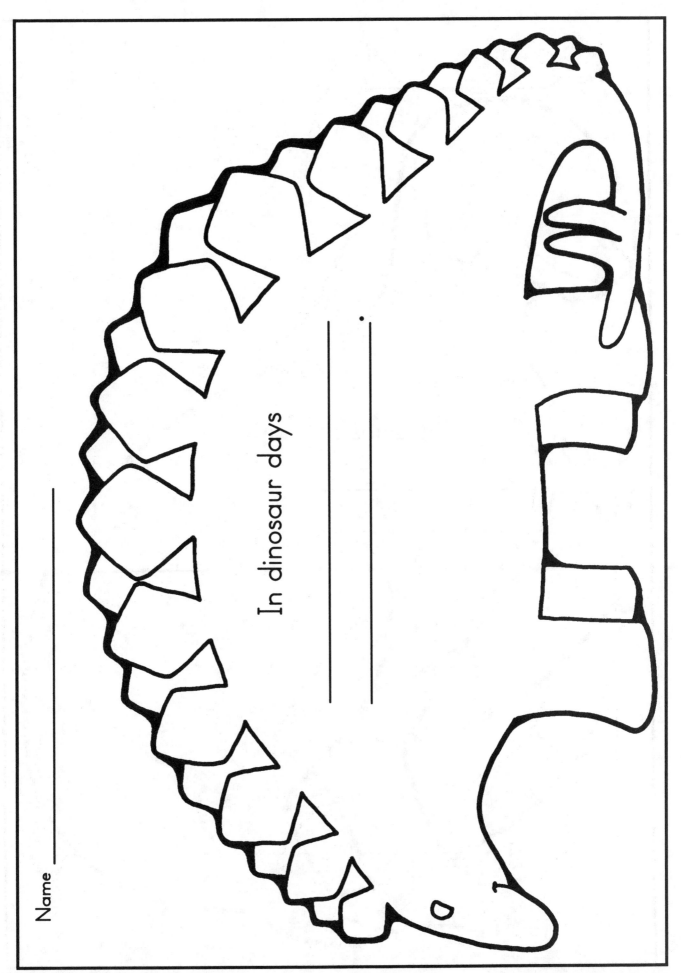

In dinosaur days

Name _____

Name _____

In dinosaur days

_____

_____ .

Name _____

Some dogs bark very loudly.
Some do not.
What kind of dog would you like?

The Letter E

I Like to Eat...

Objective: Recognize **Ee** and the long e vowel sound; discuss foods.

Motivation: Look at pictures of foods and name them. Discuss students' food likes and dislikes.

Written Expression: Students will complete the following sentence pattern on page 23:

I like to eat _____.

Illustration: Students can draw the foods they like to eat on plates within place settings (page 23).

Publication: Compile the students' work into a big book with a place setting on its cover.

Reading Skills: Write word cards for the sentence pattern and for foods the students name.

Babar, the Elephant

Objective: Recognize **Ee** and the short e sound; read "Babar" stories.

Motivation: Listen to "Babar" stories written by Laurent de Brunhoff.

Written Expression: Students can either create new Babar stories or retell their favorites, using page 24.

Illustration: Students will draw pictures to illustrate Babar stories.

Publication: Compile the students' work into a big book with Babar depicted on the cover.

Reading Skills: Write word cards for "Babar" titles, short e sound words, and other frequently used words.

Name

I like to eat

Babar, the Elephant _____

_____

The Letter F

Frog's Fun

Objective: Recognize **Ff** and its sound; study frogs.

Motivation: Students will listen to nonfiction stories about frogs. Discuss the frog's life cycle, food, protection, and enemies.

Written Expression: Students dictate a progressive "secret" story, beginning with a tadpole and continuing through a frog's adventures (page 26). The secret is that each child contributes an addition to the story but knows only the event that immediately proceeds the one which he/she is contributing. The class will know the whole story only at the end of this activity when you read it to the class. Encourage the use of words with the f sound.

Illustration: Students draw pictures to illustrate their contributions to the secret story.

Publication: Compile the students' work in sequence and bind the story into a big book with a frog on its cover.

Reading Skills: Write word cards for the following words: frog, fun, food, fish, friend, found, fast, front, for, fly, and any other f words used.

Farm Animals

Objective: Recognize **Ff** and its sound; study farm animals.

Motivation: Students listen to stories about farm animals. Brainstorm and list animals that can be seen on a farm.

Written Expression: Students complete the following pattern on page 27:

Farm animals live in barns.

They_____.

Illustration: Students draw farm animals to accompany the sentence pattern.

Publication: Compile the students' work in a barn-shaped big book. Write words under an opening window and draw animals under an opening door, using the pattern on page 28.

Reading Skills: Write word cards for names of farm animals and any words with the f sound.

Name _____

Frog's Fun

_____
_____
_____
_____

Name _____

Farm animals live in barns.
They_____.

Teacher's Page

Directions: Reproduce and cut along the dotted lines. Add flaps to the door and window which can be lifted to reveal the students' work.

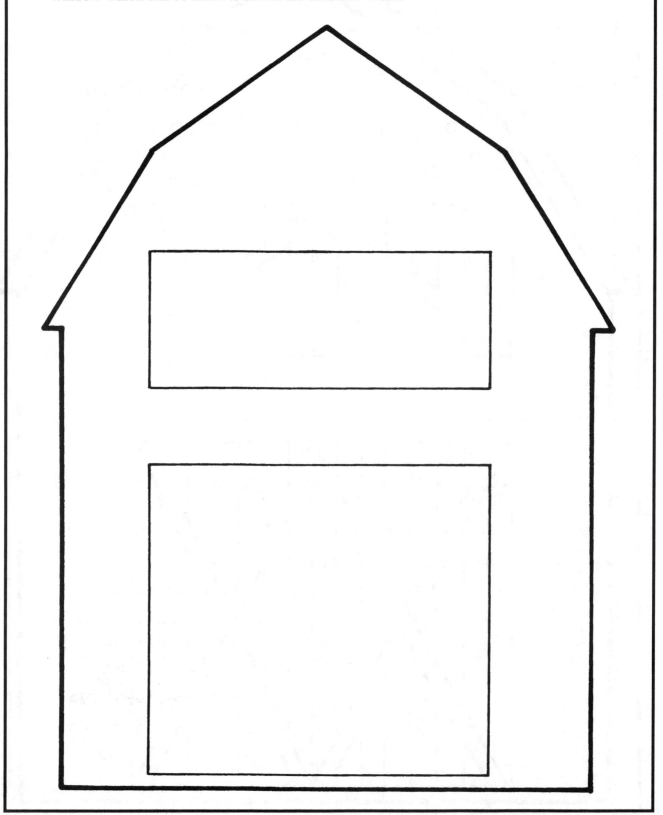

The Letter G

In My Garden

Objective: Recognize **Gg** and its sound; learn about the plants found in a garden.

Motivation: Display pictures of fruits and vegetables and discuss their growth cycle.

Written Expression: Students will complete the following sentence pattern (page 30):

> In my garden I will grow
> Lots of ___ in a row.

Illustration: Direct students to draw gardens which include their chosen plants.

Publication: Compile the students' work into a big book with a garden scene on its cover. On the final page of the big book, create a picture of your class standing in rows. Add the following sentence:

> In my class (or kindergarten) I will grow
> Lots of children in a row.

Reading Skills: Write word cards for each word in the sentence pattern. For more advanced readers, add word cards with the names of plants.

When I Grow Up

Objective: Recognize **Gg** and its sound; learn about careers.

Motivation: Students will listen to *The Growing Up, Up, Up Book* by Veronica Buffington. Brainstorm and list occupations.

Written Expression: Students will complete the following sentence pattern (page 31):

> When I grow up, I want to be a ___.

Illustration: Students will illustrate persons performing the roles of their chosen occupations.

Publication: Compile the students' work into a big book with student-drawn workers on its cover.

Reading Skills: Write a sentence strip, using the sentence pattern and accompanying word cards of chosen occupations.

Name _____

In my garden I will grow
Lots of _____ in a row.

Name_____

When I grow up,
I want to be a _____.

The Letter H

If I Had a Hat

Objective: Recognize **Hh** and its sound; discuss hats.

Motivation: Students listen to *Martin's Hats* by Joan W. Blos and *Old Hat-New Hat* by Stan and Jan Berenstain. Name and list hats associated with various jobs or activities. Ask students to bring hats from home and wear them on "Hat Day."

Written Expression: Students will complete the following sentence pattern on page 33:

If I had a _____'s hat, I would _____.

Illustration: Students can draw people wearing hats and performing the activity associated with that hat.

Publication: Compile the students' work into a big book with a cover displaying various hats.

Reading Skills: Write word cards for the book titles and for the names of hats.

This Is the House

Objective: Recognize **Hh** and its sound; compare and contrast a traditional rhyme with a modern version.

Motivation: Students listen to the traditional rhyme "This Is the House that Jack Built" and a modern version, *This Is the House Where Jack Lives* by Joan Heibroner.

Written Expression: Students will complete the following sentence pattern on page 34:

This is the _____ that _____ in the house where _____ lives.

Illustration: Provide students with art paper and a copy of page 34. The door can be cut and folded to reveal an item which they have drawn on art paper. The two sheets should be glued together.

Publication: Compile the students' work into a house-shaped big book.

Reading Skills: Write sentence strips using sections of the sentence pattern.

 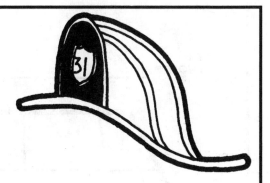

Name _____

If I had a _____'s hat,
I would _____.

Name _____

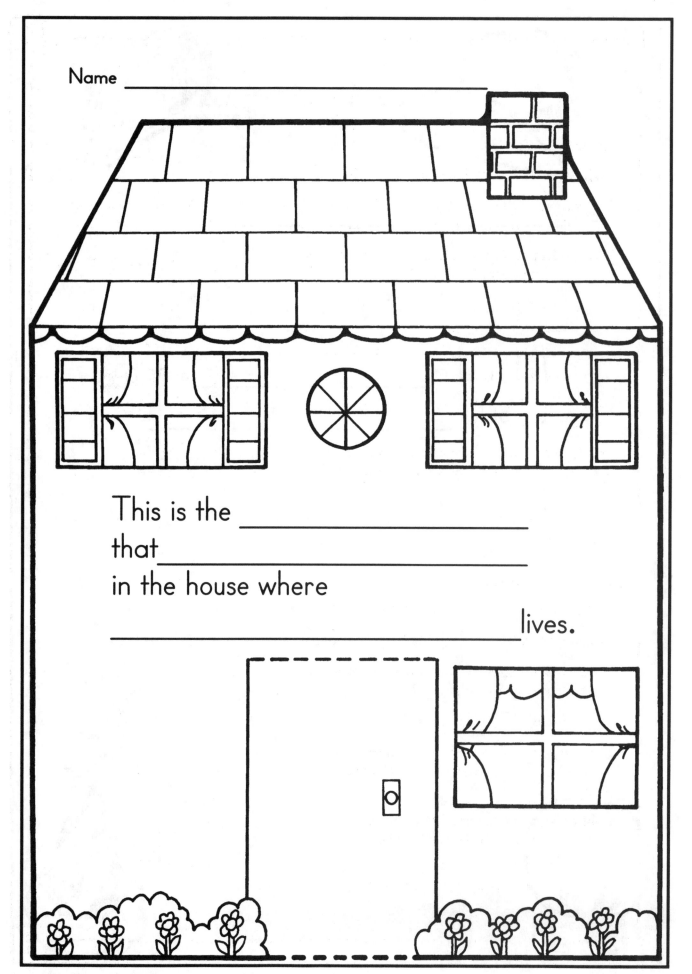

This is the _____

that _____

in the house where

_____ lives.

34

The Letter I

Insect Is My Name

Objective: Recognize **Ii** and its short i vowel sound; study insects.

Motivation: Students will listen to books about insects and name the insects pictured. The children sing "Insect Song" to the tune of "Farmer in the Dell."

Written Expression: Students substitute an insect name for the word "insect" in the following song (page 36):

> I am a/an _____
> I came from an egg,
> With wings, antennae, three body parts
> and six legs.

Illustration: Students draw an insect named in the pattern song.

Publication: Compile the students' work into a big book with insects, grass, and flowers on the cover.

Reading Skills: Write sentence strips for phrases in the song and word cards for different insects.

I Like Ice Cream

Objective: Recognize **Ii** and its long i sound; discuss ice cream.

Motivation: Students name and list flavors of ice cream and eat some ice cream.

Written Expression: Students will complete this sentence pattern on page 37:

> I like _____ ice cream.

Illustration: Students will color copies of the ice cream scoop on page 37 to match their favorite flavors.

Publication: Compile the students' "scoops" into an ice-cream-cone-shaped big book. Scoops will flip from the top.

Reading Skills: Write word cards for I, like, ice, and cream.

Name _____

I am a/an _____

I came from an egg,

With wings, antennae, three body parts

and six legs.

Name _____

I like _____ ice cream.

The Letter J

Jelly Bean Rhyme

Objective: Recognize **Jj** and its sound; name pairs of rhyming words.

Motivation: Display a jar of jelly beans. Ask students to estimate the number of jelly beans in the jar and then count them. Then, ask the students to name the colors and create a graph showing which colors are favorites. Finally, eat the jelly beans!

Written Expression: Working either individually or in a group, direct students to complete the following rhyme pattern (p. 39):

A, B, C, D, E, jelly beans!
F, G, H, I, J, _____!
K, L, M, N, O, _____!
P, Q, R, S, T, _____!
U, V, W, X, Y, _____!
Z, Z, Z, Z, Z, _____!

Illustration: Ask for volunteers to illustrate lines from the rhyme and the cover page.

Publication: Compile the rhymes and drawings into a big book with a jelly bean jar on its cover.

Reading Skills: Write sentence strips for each line of the rhyme. Write word cards for jelly beans and any words used in the rhyme.

Jack and the Beanstalk

Objective: Recognize **Jj** and its sound; recognize the final k sound; recall the sequence of a fairy tale.

Motivation: Students will listen to "Jack and the Beanstalk." Ask students to recall the story sequence.

Written Expression: Students will choose one story event to retell in their own words (page 40).

Illustration: Students will illustrate their chosen story scenes.

Publication: Collect the students' work and collate it in sequential order. Duplicate pages can be used for the big book cover and title page.

Reading Skills: Write word cards for each word in the story title. Write sentence strips for repetitive phrases.

Name _____

Jelly Bean Rhyme

A, B, C, D, E, jelly beans!

F, G, H, I, J, _____!

K, L, M, N, O, _____!

P, Q, R, S, T, _____!

U, V, W, X, Y. _____!

Z, Z, Z, Z, Z, _____!

Name _____

Jack and the Beanstalk

_____
_____
_____
_____
_____

The Letter K

Kangaroo Rhyme

Objective: Recognize **Kk** and its sound; recognize rhyming words.

Motivation: Students will listen to stories about kangaroos. They will also recite "One, Two, Buckle My Shoe," substituting the word "kangaroo."

Written Expression: Students will complete the following rhyme pattern (page 42) as a group or individually.

> One, two, kangaroo. Three, four ___.
> Five, six ___. Seven, eight ____.
> Nine, ten _____. The end.

Illustration: Student volunteers can illustrate each phrase of the rhyme.

Publication: Place rhymes and drawings in a kangaroo-shaped big book. Write the numerical forms of the numbers by the number words.

Reading Skills: Write word cards for kangaroo, kicks, other k words used, and number words. Place cards in a pocket on a kangaroo shape.

"Three Little Kittens" and Other Silly Rhymes

Objective: Recognize **Kk** and its sound; recognize rhyming words.

Motivation: Students listen to "The Three Little Kittens."

Then, ask them to recite and dramatize the nursery rhyme. Students can brainstorm a list of other animals that appear in familiar rhymes.

Written Expression: Students can choose an animal and complete the following rhyme on page 43:

> The three little _____
> lost their _____.

(Examples are moles-holes, foxes-boxes, bees-threes, fishes-dishes, and skunks-bunks.)

Illustration: Pupils illustrate their rhymes.

Publication: Compile the students' work into a big book with three kittens on the cover.

Reading Skills: Write sentence strips for the pattern and word cards for animal names.

Name _____

One, two, kangaroo.
Three, four, _____.
Five, six, _____.
Seven, eight, _____.
Nine, ten, _____.
The end.

Name _____

Three Little Kittens
and Other Silly Rhymes

The three little _____
lost their _____.

The Letter L

If I Had a Magic Lamp

Objective: Recognize **Ll** and its sound; discuss wishes.

Motivation: Listen to a story about Aladdin. Brainstorm three wishes.

Written Expression: Students complete the following pattern on page 45:

If I had a magic lamp, I would wish for ___, ____, and ____.

Illustration: Students complete the lamp pattern on page 45 and draw three wishes inside the "smoke puffs."

Publication: Compile the students' work into a big book with a magic lamp on its cover.

Reading Skills: Write word cards for the words in the sentence pattern.

I Like Lemonade

Objective: Recognize **Ll** and its sound; create a non-rhyming poem, "Lemonade."

Motivation: Follow a recipe with simple words and rebus pictures and then make and drink lemonade.

Written Expression: Students complete the following pattern on page 46:

> I like lemonade.
> It has _____.
> I like lemonade.
> It is _____.

Illustration: Student volunteers can draw pictures to match the pattern.

Publication: Compile the students' poems into a big book with lemons and a pitcher of lemonade on the cover.

Reading Skills: Write the following word cards: lemonade, lemons, like, it, I, is, and has.

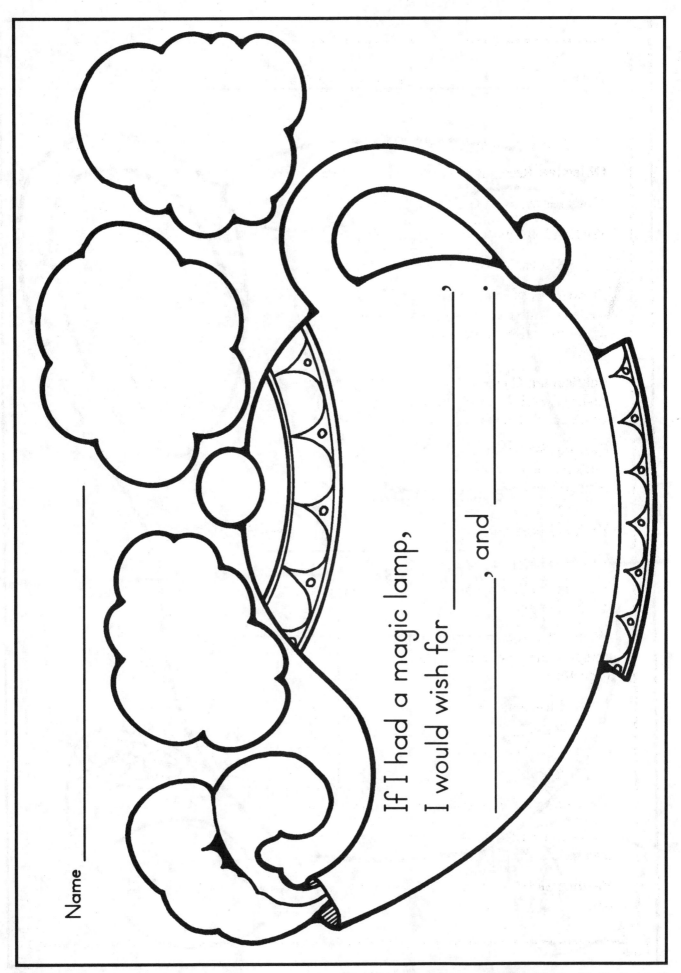

If I had a magic lamp,
I would wish for _____, and _____.

Name _____

Name _____

I like lemonade.
It has _____.
I like lemonade.
It is _____.

The Letter M

Our Monster Book

Objective: Recognize **Mm** and its sound; listen to monster stories.

Motivation: Students will listen to monster stories such as *The Monster at the End of this Book* by Jon Stone, *Meet My Pet Monster* by William McCay, and *The Monster Under My Bed* by Suzanne Gruber.

Written Expression: Students will complete the following sentence patterns on page 48:

This is _____'s monster.

It will _____.

It eats _____.

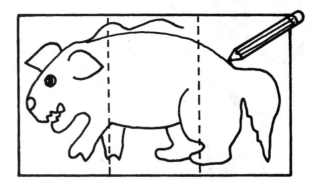

Illustration: Students can draw monsters across a page that has been divided into three sections corresponding to the head, mid-section, and tail (page 48).

Publication: Compile monsters into a flip book by cutting monsters into three sections. Student pictures and stories can be mixed and matched.

Reading Skills: Write sentence strips to match the sentence pattern

Curious George's Monkey Business.

Objective: Recognize **Mm** and its sound; become familiar with the "Curious George" story collection.

Motivation: Students will listen to H. A. Rey's "Curious George" stories and then brainstorm and list new adventures for Curious George.

Written Expression: Students will complete the story starter on page 49:

This is George.

He is a good monkey, but he is very curious.

One day, _____.

Illustration: Students can illustrate the adventures they composed about Curious George. A monkey can be duplicated. Students add background to match the story.

Publication: Compile the students' stories and drawings into a big book with Curious George on its cover.

Reading Skills: Write sentence strips for the story starter.

Name _____

This is _____'s _____ monster.

It will _____.

It eats _____.

Name _____

This is George.
He is a good monkey,
but he is very curious.
One day, _____

_____

The Letter N

The Noise Book

Objective: Recognize **Nn** and its sound; discuss things that make noise.

Motivation: Students will listen to *Splish-Splash Sounds* by Richard Scarry and *The Ear Book* by Al Perkins. Brainstorm and list things that make noises and situations in which the noises occurred.

Written Expression: Students will complete this pattern on page 51:

I heard a noise.

It was a _____.

_____, _____.

Example: bong, bong; tick, tock; clickety, clack.

Illustration: Students can illustrate the sentence pattern.

Publication: Compile the students' work into a big book with a cover depicting a silly face with big ears.

Reading Skills: Write sentence strips for the sentence pattern. Write word cards for the noises named.

No. Never...

Objective: Recognize **Nn** and its sound; begin recognition of alphabetical order and beginning sounds from a to z.

Motivation: Students listen to "An ABC of Don'ts" by Sallie Anne Rowe, which can be found in *Splendid Journey* published by Scott Foresman.

Written Expression: Students will complete the following sentence pattern on page 52 by naming an animal or object that begins with their assigned letter, along with an action that should never occur.

    A No. Never ask an alligator.
    B No. Never blow on a bear.
    C No. Never comb a cat.

Illustration: Students can illustrate the animals or objects named on the pattern or draw a person with a speech balloon saying, "No. Never . . . "

Publication: Compile the students' work into a big book with a cover displaying a drawing of people saying, "No. Never . . . "

Reading Skills: Write word cards for the book title and a card for each letter of the alphabet.

Name _____

I heard a noise.
It was a _____.

_____, _____.

Name _____

A B C D E F G H I J K L M N

No. Never _____

O P Q R S T U V W X Y Z

The Letter O

Deep in the Ocean

Objective: Recognize **Oo** and the long o vowel sound; find out about ocean and sea life.

Motivation: Students will listen to stories and name pictures of sea animals.

Written Expression: Students will complete the following pattern on page 54:

> Deep in the ocean
> I can see
> a (n)_____
> swimming in the sea.

Illustration: Students can draw a sea animal to accompany the sentence pattern.

Publication: Compile the students' work into a big book with an ocean scene on the cover.

Reading Skills: Write sentence strips of the pattern. Write word cards of the animals students named.

If I Had Eight Arms

Objective: Recognize **Oo** and the short o vowel sound; learn about an octopus; recognize number words.

Motivation: Students will brainstorm what would occur if a person had eight arms.

Written Expression: Students will complete the following pattern on page 55:

> If I had eight arms, I would _____.

Illustration: Students can illustrate what they would do if they had eight arms. Students make a handprint octopus. This is done by overlapping two handprints with fingers pointing down. Make eyes with thumbs painted black.

Publication: Compile student work into a big book with an octopus on the cover. Draw an octopus on the inside cover with section dots on the legs in combinations of one to eight. Draw lines the length of the word cards of the pattern for matching on inside cover.

Reading Skills: Write word cards for octopus, the sentence pattern, and number words from one to eight.

Name _____

Deep in the ocean I can see
a (n) _____ swimming in the sea.

Name _____

If I had eight arms, I would _____

_____ .

The Letter P

Color Poems

Objective: Recognize **Pp** and its sound; listen to poetry containing color words.

Motivation: Students will listen to poems from a book such as *I Can Fly* by Brod Badget.

Written Expression: Students will complete the non–rhyming poem on page 57. Here is an example:

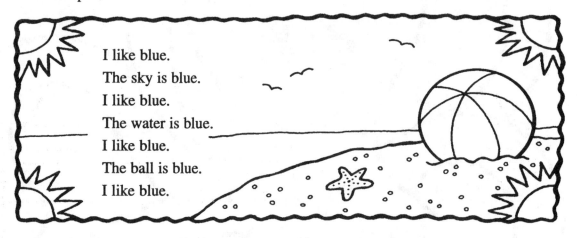

I like blue.
The sky is blue.
I like blue.
The water is blue.
I like blue.
The ball is blue.
I like blue.

Illustration: Students can draw the items named in their color poems.

Publication: Compile the students' work into a big book with a cover displaying colored balloons.

Reading Skills: Write word cards for I, like, the, is, and color words.

Winnie-the-Pooh and Pals

Objective: Recognize **Pp** and its sound; introduce "Winnie-the-Pooh" stories.

Motivation: Students will listen to "Winnie-the-Pooh" stories by A. A. Milne. While holding stuffed animals from "Winnie-the-Pooh," students will brainstorm new stories for the characters.

Written Expression: Students can create new Winnie-the-Pooh stories or retell a favorite story on page 58.

Illustration: Students draw pictures to illustrate Winnie-the-Pooh stories on page 58.

Publication: Compile students' work into a big book with Winnie-the-Pooh on the cover.

Reading Skills: Write word cards for Pooh, Piglet, pals, and any other p words used.

Name _____

Color Poem

I like _____ .
The _____ is _____ .
I like _____ .
The _____ is _____ .
I like _____ .
The _____ is _____ .
I like _____ .

Name _____

Winnie-the-Pooh and his pals _____

_____.

The Letter Q

Kings and Queens

Objective: Recognize **Qq** and its sound; listen to tales about kings and queens.

Motivation: Students will listen to a fairy tale about a king and queen such as "Snow White" or "Sleeping Beauty."

Written Expression: Students will complete the following story starter on page 60 or 61 to express what they would do if they were made king or queen:

> Once upon a time there was a (king or queen) named (child's name).
> (He or She) _____.

Illustration: Provide students with a large cutout of a Q or K to which they can glue eyes, mouth, hair, crown, and collar.

Publication: Compile the students' work into a big book with a king and queen picture on the cover.

Reading Skills: Write word cards for king, queen, and the children's names.

I was Quiet

Objective: Recognize **Qq** and its sound; discuss quiet times.

Motivation: Students will brainstorm and list situations when quiet is appropriate.

Written Expression: Students will complete the open-ended sentence on page 62.

> "I am quiet _____."

Illustration: Students can illustrate times when they are quiet.

Publication: Compile students' work into a big book with a cartoon character holding a finger to its lips and saying, "Sh! Quiet!"

Reading Skills: Write word cards for I, am, and quiet.

Name _____

Once upon a time there was a queen named

_____ Quinn _____ . She _was very a very_

quiet queen _____ .

Name _____

Once upon a time there was a king named
_____. He _____

_____.

Name _____

I am quiet _____.

Sh! Quiet!

The Letter R

Our Riddle Book

Objective: Recognize **Rr** and its sound; make up riddles.

Motivation: Hide some small objects in a container. Describe an object in riddle form and let the children guess what it might be. Students can then take turns making up riddles about animals, objects, or foods for others to guess.

Written Expression: Children will describe something in riddle form on page 64.

Illustration: Students can illustrate the answer to the riddle on the back of the page.

Publication: Compile the students' riddles into a big book with question marks of different colors and sizes on the cover.

Reading Skills: Write word cards for it, is, a, what, and the question mark.

"Somewhere Over the Rainbow, Dreams Come True"

Objective: Recognize **Rr** and its sound; discuss rainbows, colors, and dreams.

Motivation: Students will sing the song "Somewhere Over the Rainbow." Discuss their hopes and dreams.

Written Expression: Students complete the open-ended sentence on page 65, "My dream is _____." Draw a picture under the rainbow.

Illustration: Students can draw and color a rainbow.

Publication: Compile students' work into a big book with a rainbow on the cover.

Reading Skills: Write word cards for rainbow and a variety of color words.

Name _____

_____

_____

_____

What
is it?

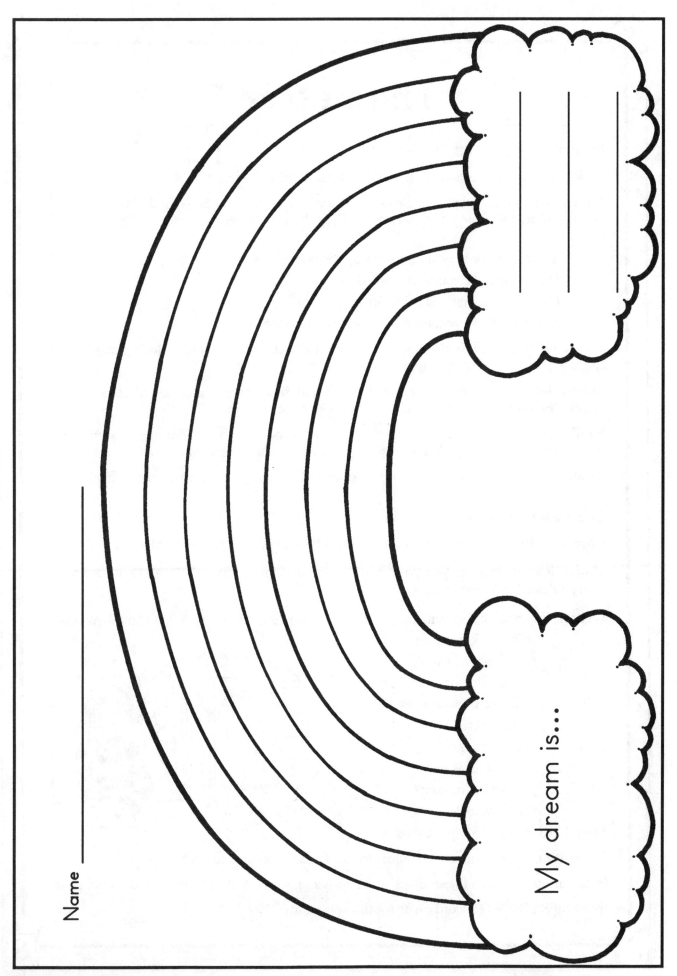

My dream is....

Name

The Letter S

Spider Rhymes and Stories

Objective: Recognize **Ss** and its sound; find out about spiders.

Motivation: Students listen to *Be Nice to Spiders* by Margaret Bloy Graham. Then, discuss spider facts and tell experiences. Sing, "Eency, Weency Spider." The words follow:

> The eency, weency spider went up the water spout,
>
> Down came the rain and washed the spider out . . .
>
> Out came the sun and dried up all the rain,
>
> And the eency, weency spider went up the spout again.

Written Expression: Students will compose original, fictional spider stories, nonfictional episodes, or rhymes, using page 67.

Illustration: Students can draw a spider web with black crayon and make a spider with a thumbprint. Add legs and face to the thumbprint with crayon.

Publication: Compile the students' work into a big book with a spider and its web on the cover. The song "Eency, Weency Spider" is written inside the cover.

Reading Skills: Write sentence strips for lines of the song "Eency, Weency Spider."

The Latchkey Kid Learns Safety

Objective: Recognize **Ss** and its sound; learn how to be safe at home alone.

Motivation: Students make a puppet in the shape of the latchkey kid, to use in naming safety rules when home alone.

Written Expression: Students respond to the following questions: What should you do if

> . . . someone knocks on your door?
>
> . . . the telephone rings?
>
> . . . you are sick or hurt?
>
> . . . someone tries to break in?
>
> . . . a fire starts?
>
> . . . you get hungry?
>
> . . . the weather is bad?
>
> . . . you get hot or cold?
>
> . . . glass breaks?

Then, have students complete page 68.

Illustration: Have students volunteer to illustrate the answer to each question.

Publication: Compile the students' work into a big book with a latchkey kid on the cover.

Reading Skills: Write word cards for the key words.

Name _____

The eency, weency spider

_____ .

Name _____

The latchkey kid
knows safety.

He or she

_____.

The Letter T

Our Transportation Book

Objective: Recognize **Tt** and its sound; recognize the tr blend; learn about transportation vehicles.

Motivation: Students will listen to books on transportation and then brainstorm and list transportation vehicles.

Written Expression: Students will complete the following sentence patterns on page 70:

I took a trip in/on a _____.

I saw _____.

I had fun traveling in a _____.

Illustration: Students can draw a chosen transportation vehicle with crayons or markers.

Publication: Compile the students' work into an accordion book by taping pages side by side and folding them like a fan. Display the book fanned open on a table or shelf.

Reading Skills: Write word cards for transportation, trip, train, truck, traveling, took, and any other t sound words.

I Had a Loose Tooth

Objective: Recognize **Tt** and its sound; learn about dental care.

Motivation: Students listen to rhyme "I Had a Loose Tooth, Wiggly Jiggly Loose Tooth." Discuss dental care. Have students describe loose teeth experiences.

Written Expression: Students will complete the open-ended story from page 71 or 72:

I had a loose tooth. I _____.

or

If I had a loose tooth, I would_____.

Illustration: Students can draw their experiences of losing teeth.

Publication: Compile the students' work into a big book with a cover displaying a cartoon face of a boy and girl with missing teeth. Write the "I Had a Loose Tooth" rhyme inside the front cover.

Reading Skills: Write sentence strips displaying sections of the "I Had a Loose Tooth" rhyme.

Name _____

I took a trip on/in a _____.

I saw _____.

I had fun traveling in a _____.

Name _____

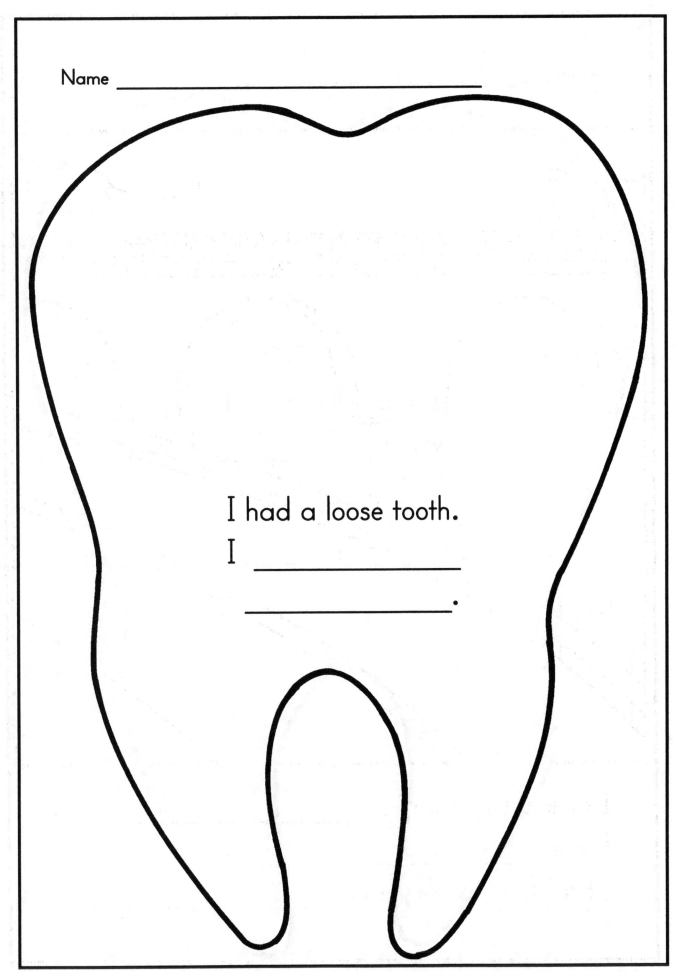

I had a loose tooth.
I _____

_____.

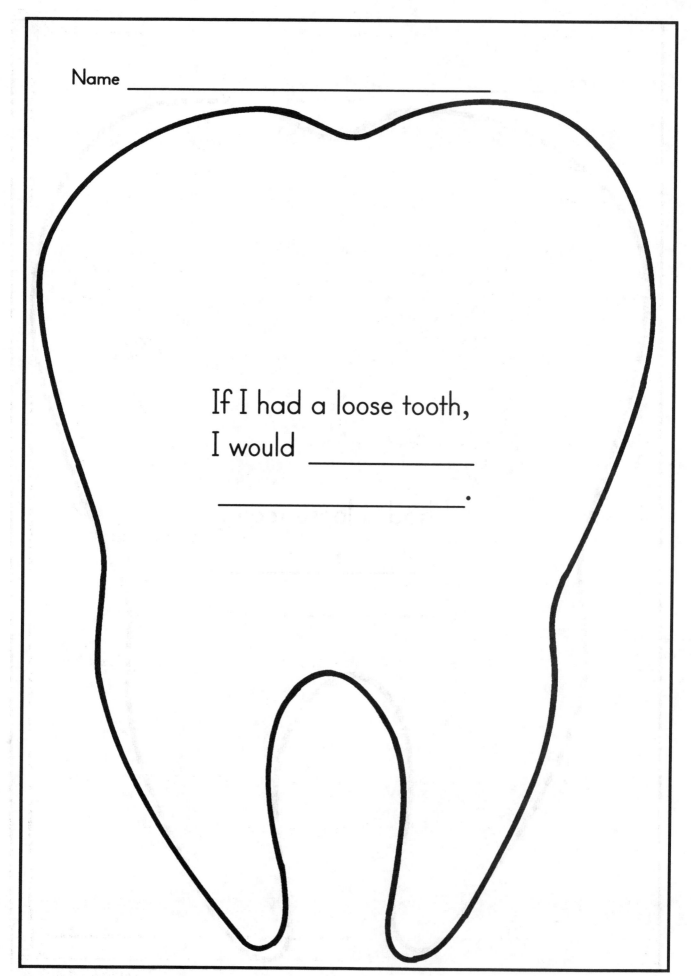

Name _____

If I had a loose tooth,
I would _____
_____.

The Letter U

I Saw a Magical Unicorn

Objective: Recognize **Uu** and the long u sound; learn about unicorns.

Motivation: Students listen to "Morgan" books by Stephen Cosgrove and "Whisper" books by Christopher Brown.

Written Expression: Students will complete the story starter on page 74, "I saw a magical unicorn."

Illustration: Students can either draw unicorns freehand, or you can provide a duplicated unicorn outline for students to color. Direct students to add a creative background scene.

Publication: Compile the students' work into a big book with a rainbow-colored unicorn on the cover.

Reading Skills: Write word cards for I, saw, a magical, unicorn.

What Is Up?

Objective: Recognize **Uu** and the short u vowel sound; study the preposition up.

Motivation: Students listen to *Great Day for Up* by Dr. Seuss and then brainstorm and list things that are up.

Written Expression: Students will complete the following sentence pattern on page 75:

What is up?

A _____ is up.

Illustration: Students can illustrate the items they named in the pattern.

Publication: Compile the students' work into a big book with a colorful arrow pointing up on the cover.

Reading Skills: Write word cards for the pattern and student-chosen words.

Name _____

I saw a magical unicorn.

_____

_____

_____

_____

_____

Name _____

What is up?

A _____ is up.

The Letter V

The Very Violet Van

Objective: Recognize **Vv** and its sound; study and discuss pictures of violet-colored objects.

Motivation: Students will listen to *Teeny Tiny* by Jill Bennett, becoming familiar with its predictable pattern. Then, students will brainstorm and list objects that are violet.

Written Expression: Students will complete the following pattern on page 76:

Once there was a very violet van,

and in the very violet van there was a very violet _____.

Illustration: Students can draw an outline of the violet object they named on page 76. When finished, you can cut out the interior of the drawing.

Publication: Compile the students' work in the middle section of a tri-fold big book with a violet van on the cover or first fold. On the back of the third section, glue a large violet heart cut from velvet or other lush material so that it shows through the students' cutout pictures (see page 78).

Reading Skills: Write word cards for very, violet, velvet, van, and valentine.

A Volcano Is...

Objective: Recognize **Vv** and its sound; learn more about volcanoes.

Motivation: Students will look at books and pictures of volcanoes and discuss volcano facts. Then, students will brainstorm and list words describing volcanoes inside a large outline of a volcano.

Written Expression: Students will complete the pattern on page 79:

A volcano is _____.

Illustration: Students can draw a volcano with crayons or markers.

Publication: Compile the students' work into a big book with a volcano on its cover.

Reading Skills: Make word cards for the pattern and words named in describing volcanoes.

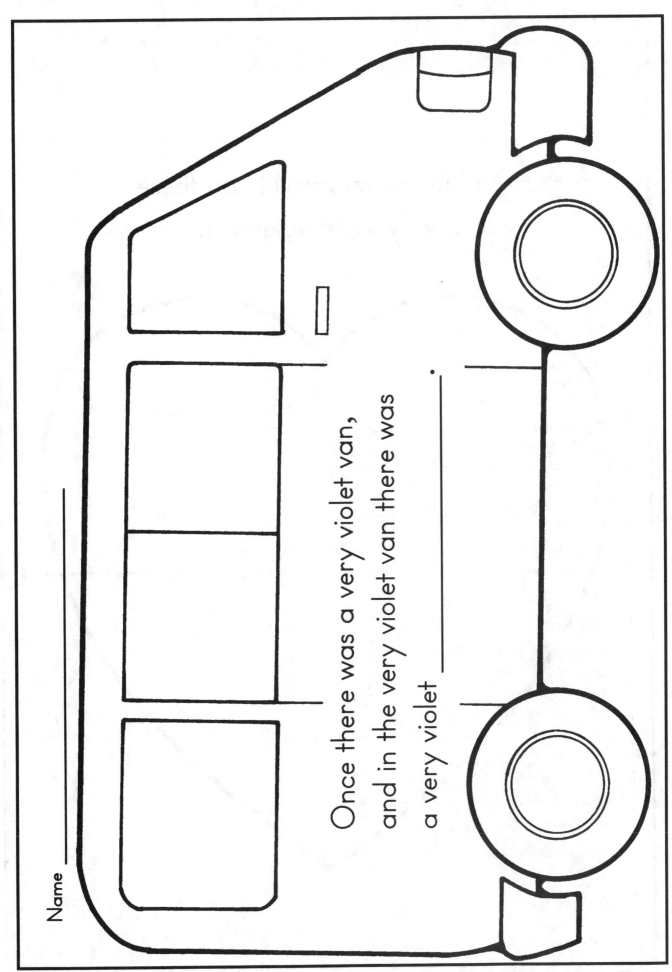

Name _____

Once there was a very violet van,
and in the very violet van there was
a very violet _____

And in the very violet van there was a very violet valentine.

Name _____

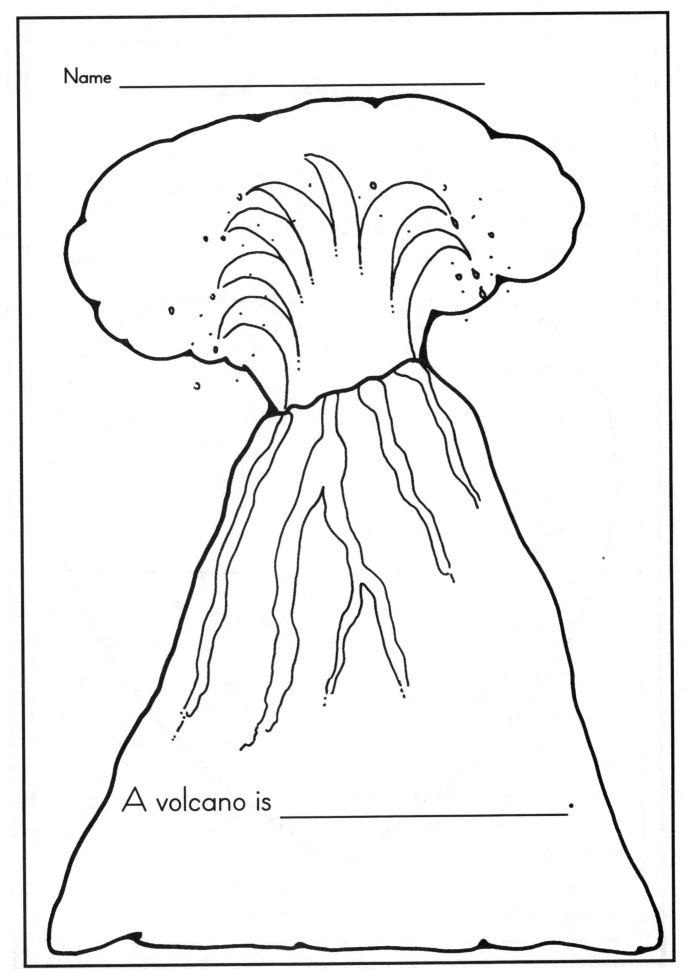

A volcano is _____.

The Letter W

Pig with Wig and Other Wacky Rhymes

Objective: Recognize **Ww** and its sound; construct simple rhymes.

Motivation: Students will brainstorm and list names of animals with rhyming words. Examples include bees/peas, fox/box, owl/towel, cat/mat, duck/truck, etc.

Written Expression: Students will name an animal with a corresponding rhyming word (page 81).

Illustration: Students can draw pictures of their chosen animals and rhyming words.

Publication: Compile the students' work into a big book with pig and wig on the cover.

Reading Skills: Write word cards for pig with wig, wacky, and other rhyming word pairs.

Wolf Stories

Objective: Recognize **Ww** and its sound; recognize fairy tales with wolves as the central characters.

Motivation: Students will listen to the following stories.

- "Little Red Riding Hood"
- "The Three Little Pigs"
- "Peter and the Wolf"
- "The Boy Who Cried Wolf"
- "The Wolf and the Seven Kids"

These stories are excellent for dramatization. Consider video taping the students' plays and having the tape available for check-out with the big book.

Written Expression: Students will complete the following sentence on page 82:

My favorite wolf story is _____.

Illustration: Students can illustrate their favorite wolf stories.

Publication: Compile the students' work into a big book with a wolf on its cover.

Reading Skills: Write phrase strips of the names of wolf stories.

Name _____

Pig with Wig and
Other Wacky Rhymes

_____ with _____

Name _____

My favorite wolf story is _____

_____.

The Letter X

Open the Box

Objective: Recognize **Xx** and its ending sound; name objects found in a box.

Motivation: Students will listen to *Don't Open This Box* by James Razzi. Students will then brainstorm and list things that can be found inside a box.

Written Expression: Students will complete the following rhyme on page 84:

> I opened a box
> and what did I see?
> A _____
> was in it for me!

Illustration: Students can draw pictures of objects inside the box shape on page 84. You may wish to have students attach paper lids that can flip open to display the objects.

Publication: Compile the students' work into a big book shaped like a box.

Reading Skills: Write word cards for the predictable rhyme pattern.

If I Had X-Ray Vision

Objective: Recognize **Xx** and its beginning sound; explore the concept of imagination.

Motivation: Students will brainstorm and list what could be accomplished if a person had X-ray vision. Censor any unacceptable answers!

Written Expression: Students will complete the following open-ended phrase on page 85:

> If I had X-ray vision, I could _____.

Illustration: Students will color the X-ray glasses and draw what would happen if they had X-ray vision. See page 85.

Publication: Compile the students' work into a big book with a picture of X-ray glasses on its cover.

Reading Skills: Write reading cards for the pattern sentence.

Name _____

I opened a box
and what did I see?
A _____
was in it for me!

84

Name _____

If I had X-ray vision,
I could _____
_____ .

The Letter Y

Yes, I Had Manners

Objective: Recognize **Yy** and its beginning sound; recognize and use polite words and phrases associated with good manners.

Motivation: Students will listen to *Thank-you, Excuse Me,* and other good manners books by <u>Janet Richecky</u>. They will also listen to *Please, Thank-You* by Richard Scarry. Students will then brainstorm and list polite words.

Written Expression: Students will complete the following sentence pattern (page 87):

Yes, I had manners when ___.

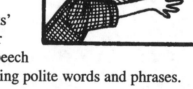

Illustration: Students will illustrate on page 87 a situation in which they used good manners. You may wish to show students how to use a speech balloon.

Publication: Compile the students' work into a big book with a cover displaying happy children with speech balloons over their heads, containing polite words and phrases.

Reading Skills: Write word cards for polite words and phrases.

What Is Yellow?

Objective: Recognize **Yy**; examine pictures of yellow objects.

Motivation: Students will brainstorm and list things that are yellow.

Written Expression: Students will complete the following sentence pattern on page 88:

Yellow is _____.

Illustration: Students can use yellow fingerpaint to create pictures of their yellow objects. Use other paint colors to add details.

Publication: Compile the students' work into a big book with a friendly sun on its cover.

Reading Skills: Write word cards for yellow and the yellow objects the children named.

Name _____

Yes, I had manners when

_____

_____

_____ .

#049 Making Big Books A to Z

Name _____

Yellow is _____.

The Letter Z

Zebra, Zebra, What Do You See?

Objective: Recognize **Zz** and its sound; learn facts about zoo animals.

Motivation: Students will listen to stories and facts about zoo animals. They will also listen to *Brown Bear* by Bill Martin, Jr. Finally, they will brainstorm and list zoo animals.

Written Expression: Students will complete the following sentence pattern on pages 90-95:

> Zebra, zebra what do you see?
> I see a(n)_____
> looking at me.

Illustration: Students can trace zoo animal patterns on colored construction paper. Students can use scrap construction paper to cut or tear spots, eyes, stripes, hair, grass, trees, water, sky, and sun, or they can try using a hole punch to make colored circles to use.

Publication: Compile the students' work into a big book with a zebra on its cover.

Reading Skills: Write word cards for the sentence pattern, using one color, and for zoo animals, using another color.

If I Were a Zoo Animal

Objective: Recognize **Zz** and its sound; continue learning about zoo animals.

Motivation: Students will brainstorm and list as many facts as they can about zoo animals they have already learned about.

Written Expression: Students will complete the following sentence pattern on page 96:

> If I were a(n)_____,
> this is what I would do.
> I would _____, _____, and _____.
> That is what I would do.

Students should repeat the same word for the triple blanks.

Illustration: Students draw zoo animals performing the actions they named on page 96.

Publication: Compile the students' work into a big book with zoo pictures on its cover.

Reading Skills: Write sentence strips for each phrase of the predictable pattern.

Name _____

Zebra, zebra what do you see?

Name _____

I see a _____
looking at me.

Name _____

I see a(n) _____
looking at me.

92

Name _____

I see a(n) _____
looking at me.

Name _____

I see a _____
looking at me.

Name _____

I see a _____
looking at me.

Name _____

If I were a (n)_____,
this is what I would do.
I would _____, _____, and
_____.
That is what I would do.

EDUCATION RESOURCE CENTER
UNIVERSITY OF DELAWARE